M000007085

*This is a world
very wolved*

different from yesterday's
and already begun to cool

Ahsahta Press
Boise, Idaho

2017

The New Series
#82

Gatherest

Sasha Steensen

Ahsahta Press, Boise State University, Boise, Idaho 83725-1525
Cover design by Quemadura
Book design by Janet Holmes
ahsahtapress.org

LIBRARY OF CONGRESS CATALOGING-IN-PUBLICATION DATA

Names: Steensen, Sasha, author.
Title: Gatherest / Sasha Steensen.
Description: Boise, Idaho : Ahsahta Press, 2017. | Series: The New Series ;
    #8 2 | Includes bibliographical references.
Identifiers: LCCN 2017029670| ISBN 9781934103777 (acid-free paper) | ISBN
    1934103772 (acid-free paper)
Classification: LCC PS3619.T4416 A6 2017 | DDC 811/.6—DC23
LC record available at https://lccn.loc.gov/2017029670

Contents

Erthe toc of erthe erthe wyth woh,
erthe other erthe to the earthe droh,
erthe leyde erthe in earthene throh,
tho hevede erthe of erthe erthe ynoh.

—ANONYMOUS, 12TH CENTURY

Kiss of our agony Thou gatherest,
O Hand of Fire
gatherest—

—HART CRANE

Waters

A Lenten Poem

Deep calleth unto deep at the noise of thy waterfalls:
All thy waves and thy billows are gone over me.

—PSALM 42:7

last night I had a watery dream

it broke
the flood

the good star
guided me

said, look through the hollow
& see it full

held me rapt
not in linen
but in love

I.

if found in water
wash

not a spot
on the forehead

goes
unnoticed

by woe

nor a toe
unbroken

the language
of devotion

flexible as bone

a small vessel
with one small

hole

never
overflows

I the ode
work furiously

upon fury in each
room of my home

I call out
as stones do
not to you

but to doubt
I love doubt

its firmness
when all else

falls through
it forms

the everlasting
hole

the good news
is this this
selfsame delight

3.

I go by goat
through the mountain

lion's mouth

there is no
paradise

dearer

nor further
from home

than one's own

I will boil your hooves
strengthen my bones
rest upon your coat

I will be so gentle-tender
as to shoe your foot

I forsook only
one body

my own

I reach out
my hand
& inside
your mouth
thirsty

find
thought
that cannot
exhaust

find
the gulf weed
no one
believed

only water can coil
into a shell
only water waits
wades out to the pool to greet me

5.

the creature
had a tail of water
I loved it loved it loved
it and gave it away

I have a misshapen fever
only another
can calm

him him

he addeth to it
sucking stones
so that I might mouth
something when he goes

that noah built his boat
to rest upon my tongue
means I believe

& so I tell her
Daughter
people are not bad
not evil
people want to be like water
and go where currents send them

6.

lent has come
with love to town
the limbs a joy to see
bundled up
& hauled off
by the garbage truck

even the worms woo
under clouds
even the penis
paragon of pearl
or diamond
shows me mercury
a constant bleeding
good great innermost
planet

thee

I know
I am one of those
may bells
male lilies
now
gather up your clothes

7.

who doesn't know
that all good things
are found
in holes

who doesn't crouch
down & in the crevice
find sublime
ditches in which to climb

if you gaze for long
into an abyss
the abyss gazes
back into you

& then you die
& happily

we saw so many animals
looking back
they form a tangle of limbs
heads claws and beak bones

we saw some others too

we pushed and pulled each other
in the rented wagon

none was sure
she enjoyed herself

at each cage crying
I want to see something else

it will not be long now
before the pachyderms
have a new home

humans as certain of ourselves
as we are of the animals

have our rituals

9.

no: tis a fast to dole
thy sheaf of wheat

                    and meat

unto the hungry soule

it is to fast from strife
from old debate

                    and hate

to circumcise thy life

to shew a heart grief-rent
to sterve thy sin
            not bin
and that's to keep thy lent

a zenith

when one
sees one

drops its paddle

in the canoe
holds up its palm

the river empties
unto a lake

of black

feels a relief
as it sees

mica

its reflection
in history

we eat
animate things

exhume
energy

lending words

to the smallest
of us all

II.

taking up
what no one
else wants
to carry

this is its own
kind of worship

faith
is the substance
of faith

the difference
between air
& water

the world's other body

I kneel down
to diaper it it
laughs to see me
so diapered

12.

I set my foot down in the hole I dug in darkness so no one would see

I denied you entry
I the laurel tree

If my child is killed by a gun I vow to bring the barrel to the heads of
my countrymen

& women

we do not see how we have been
complete
replete with kindness
with majesty

on this day of lent
we went to empire
over our dead

we went
wreathed with grief
& chardon thistles

we went clothed in an anger that does not let itself go easily

we went
to the barn

where our weapons are

waiting
patiently

there our heart
shall also be

13.

in the dream of dreams

the master butcher at his block separates the cut from the carcass with
his eyes shut

increasingly
his job

case-ready
& in vitro meat

repairer
of the breach

restorer
of the streets

obsolete

transformation this side of death is belief
& acknowledgment
the cousin of sin

15.

forsythia so early
before
a season

breeds anxiety

shows its
oleaceous heart

to be
full of bees

you misheard me
it wasn't *ideal*
I said
but *idea*
in its endlessness

I've been thinking
for several hours now

& for several hours before that
I worked through what to do
once the thinking was done

no one lent me
forty days

for listening

I do not give up
but give in

not to mercy

which is the same
as silence

relentless

I will not look
at your noise

not once

this afternoon

not this evening

either

& I will not
not exit

without noticing

if it exists

the thing we call
a lapse

all we know for sure

is that a physical phenomenon
is experienced
more and less so

we also know the illustrative relationship
between silhouette and shadow

the undiscovered rules
will uncover themselves

soon

then I will know what I am doing
besides mothering
losing children
& drawing conclusions

or drawing out what could be done
not in several days
but in one

18.

when women
open their mouths

and ask
for timely babies

warmth warms
them & ultimately

I have not forgotten
your ovaries

where I was carried

where I
emerged

they all remain yours

the words men use
are little wars

they warn
my girls
against opening

their bodies

are not yours
but theirs

to lord over

19.

at one point
gryll meant fierce

now
it wouldn't

the most ponderous
is to keep her stiff at sea

something that produces
a baby
a dead body
birth
the opposite of flexibility

to understand the great gift
I submerge myself
head first
in an auxiliary verb
filled with water

it was

I am

a girl

when angry
the toddler screams
"bad boy!"
at me

20.

today is the birthdays
of so many hims

who don't mean
but are so many
worlds to me

brother husband brother

entered
bloody like she

we've been writing
about fire engines

all day long
for days straight

which is to say

we've been writing
with weight and urgency

instead of waiting
for Christ's return

I should nail to my door
the words and figures
my daughter draws

these too say something
that was never said
prior to her arrival

they have their correlatives
in her world

they point straight at Eros
like an arrow

they dress themselves in joy
that looks like sorrow

22.

I put my left ear on the desk
& ask for a poem
nothing arrives
nearby

I put my right ear on my chest
& ask for a poem
where could it be

I make many things
not least among them
errors

I also dream and receive:

let us not forget
what is shallow
& what is deep
eventually meet

just as Jules Verne
comes to know

the monster
the submarine
of the soul

would not
willingly go

to see what it means
beneath

because relief is
an onion

no
the smooth innards
of an almond
along the tongue

I tongue him

I love him
his every pleats' fold

what Pliny calls
the black oak
of the tunny fish

I had thought
this was my love letter
to God
but now I see how lusty
and I wonder
if he'll have me

what surprises me is this:
feverwort weren't
of the honeysuckle family
their erect hairy round stem
fistular & therefore before
I put myself before you I say I

am certain

from everything
which we bring forth
eventually we feed

25.

in the book
of Nahum

the Lord is furious

in the book
they be folden
together
as thorns

while the book
lay open

my rind
lay open

if there be
a woman
present

fuck

means blown by the wind
otherwise to beat with a rod

the book
& the flower of Lebanon
languisheth

the book old
like a pool of water

the book
dashed in pieces
at the top of all streets

the book
like a fig tree
shaken

the book
feedingplace
of lions
of whoredoms
of cankerworms
of wellfavored harlots

the book
set as a gazingstock
like a city on a hill
like its lantern

the book says
like

the book says
goodnight

26.

on this day
of lent

we shot the black boy
in the chest

not my son
not our president
but dearly loved
nevertheless

when Christ curses the tree
fruit a hundredfold
does grow
& feeds us all

no one dares say
the morning dove's call
disrupts

no one but my gun

no one

how is it that we have forgotten
salvation means
to be
in the world
with mercy

my daughter tells her daddy:
nothing is perfect
but the thing in which
you do not believe

I call the adders to me
fig fig

no one
roasts the bird

no one
swallows water

in the spring evenings tilling

the northern flicker at my chimney cap again

within this country's jurisdiction
skunks and lobstermen

form litters

make friends

shake hands

it is a relic to wear the dead on your forehead
and yet
it is alive and well along the Ganges

it is fine to do what the Bible
says we ought to

its purpose
is its existence

ours to walk through
a thousand deserts

I guess this is
the gift given by God

time

to escape not
what might have been
but what is

29.

it is not prayer
that covers over
cowardice and envy

nothing with a tongue
can taste
or say it

& nothing with an ear
either

there are earlier versions
of the crucifixion

our urkontinent
soft as gypsum

& also spearlike

if he survives three days
he might be allowed to live

otherwise his head
a feast for the birds
and the earth
entire

I so often go there
to the damp ground
where it extends its arm
but can't quite
reach

I get on my knees

a stalk in still water
seems to breathe
seems borne of something

genitals cast upon the sea
do not become the seed of beauty
but of deceit

well inside the falls
we break our looking in half
the egg-world in tact
the yoke
darts below
& kills the very last minnow

without wetting me
God there
happens to be

31.

today
my 38th birthday
my daughter ate a walnut
& puffed up

but as if
a gift
she kept breathing
breathing

she had a shard
of pearl in her eye

he had a garland
of hides

not around his head
& so I stroked

the evenness between them
kept them
both warm
& safe from water

the moist nature of a seed
is the beginning
of things grown moist

or the growth of moist things

the globe grows warm
the sun grows behind us
& low in the sky

I nearly touch the thought
cannot exhaust it
the million spherical drops

rainbows pebbles stones weeds roots of trees

grot
is two kinds of words:
dirty & the hole into which water flows

I almost forgot
what we lost

drift of kelp and reef
stand apart from themselves

it's simple to see
in a pool of light

bird above me

I worship
the beetle & the marshreed
because of their variety

there is another kind of logic
that delights in itself
& so hopes
to bring forth
a smaller self like itself

by saying
the eye of my eye
it tries to catch
inward sight
but instead
it opens
the owl's eye
in daylight

it seems full of luck
but it's built of distrust
a kind of machine
made of swords
it hurls itself at its very self

though it is much lovelier
than this poem could ever be
I leave it to masturbate
in a patch of coltsfeet

instead I see
where water drips
the annoying constancy
I see a lumpsucker

I see the opposite of an arrow
I see men in hats eating chicken feet
I see only a fathom deep
leapt out to greet me

and in seeing
I say what I saw and fall prey
to myself in the exact same way

I can't be still
I'm here
with what makes me unkillable
though killed
like a midwife
who at dawn
has all in order

       and this is an old story

floating to light by chance
a breath
is political
this touch is political
the tangling of all our lifelines
of our human air

       the sea is another story

I forget
what year it is
I'm thinking
if I lie on the beach with you
in my rose-wet cave—
whatever happens this is

       the dream of a common language

as we live it now:
over and over
handed down
knowing   knowing   knowing
with grief with fury with action   in the wake of home

will any of this comfort you

and how should this comfort you

36.

An unreality is lent the sentence:
The chervil's long root is buried under the donkey's foot.

the strange creature
pained by love
is sweeter than a weed

I can see how the children pine
after God
how they glean all they need
from one another

she seems
never to ask a question
that doesn't
involve belief

if the river we watch
watches itself
we see a watchful stone
we do not see tides

I tried but could not find
a way to resist

what washes over us
like waters

not simply grief
but relief from grief

occurs
& ginger too
its nebulous root
& when I awake
life anew

38.

at its bottom
something older
than the world's five corners
rests

what can water offer
overripe earth
but a spume
a deflated balloon
in which to get caught

o little little
whirlpool
to whom
I am in debt
& littler gull
bereft

I assure you
lakes are
just as holy
fire & water
calm equally

welcome
to our home built
of rough-hewn stone

water is assumed
during birth
to soothe

so that so
many women
with some means
bring tubs
along with them

I had thought
my god
water

I put it in my mouth

& I mouthed it it
was more than I held
in my hand
and yet
less

I loved dying young

flushed & heartsick

I took off my clothes
knotted up
an oilcloth

balled
in a bed
of bindweed

until

the birthyell
seemed
to me
both mine
and somebody else's

I kept a certain
kind of time

mine

the insect
larger than a gnat
& smaller than a fly

flies

between me and the page

I only want to say what I mean by the page

the page
& nothing else

I feel the need
to be

quiet

inside

I Couldn't Stop Watching

For a long time, nothing came between the poems on water and the poem on fire. Neither touching nor at any visible distance, they seemed alibis for each other. It is easy now to see their failures, brilliantly shiny.

There were poems I thought to write. I returned again and again to *The Book of Fixed Stars*. The title fascinated me almost as much as the intricate double draw-ings. One from outside the celestial globe and one from inside. Swans drawn as if affixed to the sky with dissection pins, the horse's head levitating above a star chart, rabbits leaping over one another.

And then, the beautiful twins, their bodies overlapping so that I can almost see my husband and his brother in the womb, arm touching thigh.

Though I have no solid medical evidence, I believe I once had two conceptuses. The irregular pregnancy, the alarming, oddly shaped placenta, my daughter's enlarged and reddened breast. Perhaps the mole we thought we saw on sever-al ultrasounds burrowed out somehow during those early months, leaving her inconsolable until the age of two. When I ask Greta about her life in the womb, she reports warmth, and then, suddenly, its absence. Something knot, and then not, on the other side of the membrane. *Al Bakar*, the White Ox, is visible from Southern Arabia, and I will likely never see it.

But, I've left the title behind. We know that stars have a parallax, not to mention motion that is more than apparent. I kept feeling fixed stars and fits and starts. What if stars have origins, parents of sorts, and what if it is a kind of betrayal to give them new names? How are the stars' magnitudes figured, I wonder. I am sure I can find the answer to *this* question, but instead I leave it behind as well.

Abd al-Rahman al-Sufi also known as Abd ar-Rahman as-Sufi or Abd al-Rhaman Abu al-Husayn is known in the west as Azophi. I keep imagining a ferryboat carrying Azophi slowly toward me through galaxies he liked to call clouds.

He seems a beauty, and he hides his face behind black paper pierced with holes. Whether this is the veil of life or the veil of death

                                                                    remains

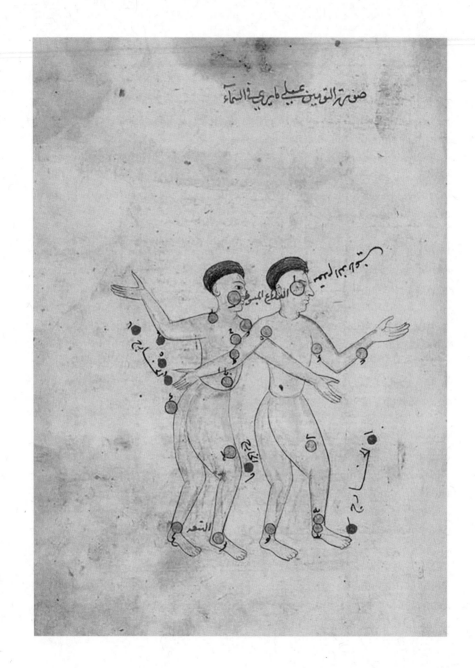

"At home" is not a container but a site and an event. The house is too small, and children regularly choose to pee in the backyard as opposed to waiting for someone to get off the pot. Bodily analogies tempt me, and while I have heard individuals say they feel they've been given the wrong body, I've never heard anyone say they've outgrown their body. And yet the house is a kind of body that seems never large enough until, perhaps, it catches up with death, or burns to the ground.

Blanchot says the I never dies, that is, the I doesn't say I am dead otherwise it would master its own death, and we all know death's master is death itself. Even when I figure an afterlife, I realize that if it has a master, it is itself itself as well. Given the difficulty we have distinguishing between consciousness put into question and consciousness of being put into question, it is futile to do anything other than tell the right kind of bedtime stories, the kind that enlarge the house and render death an inaccessible phenomena we ought not discuss at this late hour. I realize this may turn out to be an ineffective parenting technique, but I go on in hopes of comforting frightened but sleepy children.

With the children in their bunk beds, I think of writing a poem on sentence diagramming. The diagrams are as beautiful as Azophi's star charts, but words radiate more comfortably than pinned stars. I have been more than undisciplined lately, drinking in the evenings, sleeping until 7 am, riding my bike instead of reading. In their book, *Higher Lessons in English. A work on English Grammar and Composition, In which the Science of the Language is made Tributary to the Art of Expression. A Course of Practical Lessons Carefully Graded, and Adapted to Every Day Use in the School-Room,* Brainerd Kellogg and Alonzo Reed insist, "As a means of discipline nothing can compare with a training in the logical analysis of the sentence." They employ the word "fitness" in a manner entirely new to me— as in, the (eternal) fitness of things to their words, or is it words to their things?

if it flickers

(t)here

hearing a step

in that 'cleave' of being which each of his creatures shews to God's eyes alone
(Hopkins)

then

it remains

The history of the American parse tree begins not with Kellogg and Reed, but with S.W. Clark's earlier obscene balloons.

Dangling as they do from the penis of the sentence—*held*—words are stored like semen in two misshapen sacs. As is the case with many penises, small benign growths and protruding veins give this particular sentence balloon its unique shape.

And yet (at its reaches)

                        mother   And   child

Each aloft

                                    And   (afloat)

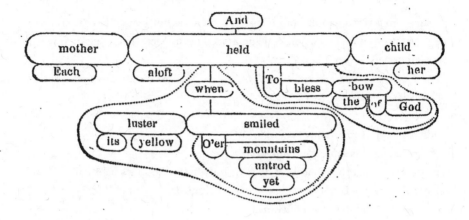

I manage to write a handful of poems on sentences, but really, they turn out to be illustrations on sentence-making, organized by subject. Here's one such poem, written in bed:

Sentences on Sadness

I admit I have been terribly sad.
While writing this sentence, I am weeping.
The danger is that the situational, slowly, but always, becomes habitual.
That awkward figure, God, made us coats of skins.
We make our children coats of skins too.
Sensical, borne as she was from nonsensical, floats above and beyond her mother.
What is left is like a mist hovering, threatening not to disappear, and threatening in
    its disappearance.
I am worried about worry, what it does to the body, to the psyche.
How it has its way with me while I sleep, while I winnow down the list,
while I wipe more asses than I own.
I was told that there are activities better done for twenty minutes every day than
    for hours once a week.
In this way, perhaps writing and exercising are akin to crying.

As far as sentences go, I fear mine are unventuresome. Eventually, the titles of the sentence poems I mean to write far outnumber those actually written.

Sentences on Contraception
Sentences on Lenten Waiting
Sentence on War

Sentences on Dreams about Nightmares

Sentences on Nightmares about Dreams

Sentences on Stealing

Sentences on Preschool

Sentences on It

Sentences on Shitting

Sentences on Seaboards

Sentences on Shapes

Sentences on Falling (off a chair, swing, hammock or bed)

Sentences on So-and-So

Sentences on Cereal

Sentences on If-Then Configurations

Sentences on Illegitimate Rape

Sentences on Husbands

                                                 & of course

Sentences on Sentences

Several centuries ago, *sentence* meant *question* and *period* meant *sentence*. *Period,* a transliteration of the Greek word *periodos* ("a way around"), was a collection of words related grammatically and semantically. Just as words within the sentence disappear into a larger notion, *period* singularizing itself via Medieval Latin, could only hold by holding together. In 1597, Calligrapher Peter Bales calls the character which signifies but sounds not "a full pricke."

that which pierces the page   also menstruates

In John Gent Smith's *The mysterie of rhetorique unveil'd wherein above 130 of the tropes and figures are severally derived from the Greek into English : together with lively definitions and variety of Latin, English, scriptural, examples, pertinent to each of them apart. Conducing very much to the right understanding of the sense of the letter of the scripture, (the want whereof occasions many dangerous errors this day). Eminently delightful and profitable for young scholars, and others of all sorts, enabling them to discern and imitate the elegancy in any author they read, &c.,* the word *hirmos*, a bond or knot, is offered as the period's twin:

a figure whereby a sudden entrance is made into a confused heap of matter

knit or coupled together

With their broken lines for coordinating conjunctions, their small x for what is not said but implied, their angled lines for participles, their hovering lines for direct address or interjections, and their tails for articles, it isn't hard to see why Kellogg and Reid's sentence diagrams take hold while Clark's balloons float away in the distance until we see, first, a prick of sky, then a trick of the eye. Beyond their reassuring symmetry, they offer a hierarchy meant to bridge belief and proper dependency.

I come to this parse tree in a "specimen copy" once held by the Library of the State Agricult'l College, Fort Collins, Colorado. As far as I can tell, I am the first patron since September 1996 to withdraw the book from Colorado State University's Storage Overflow Building. My library liaison has advised me to check out books that I would like the library to keep else their future, should they be granted one, will be digitized. In Lesson 59, Complex Sentence-Adjective Clauses, I find the following sentence eagerly awaiting diagramming:

The lever which moves the world of mind is the printing-press.

<u>Ah</u>

the word

x   the lever to which you referred

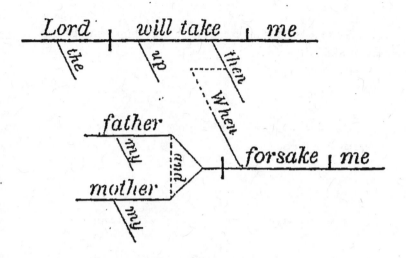

I am aware that refinement of mind and clearness of thinking usually result from grammatical studies. (Lesson 128)

&

The guilt of the slave trade, which sprang out of the traffic with Guinea, rests with John Hawkins (Lesson 59).

&

What means that hand upon the breast of thine? (Lesson 120)

Perhaps it is because I am attracted to sentences like these, all lifted from Kellogg and Reid, that I can't seem to interest myself to the same degree in today's trees, which can be parsed into a seemingly endless array of structures, some more closely resembling a razed forest than a growing tree.

William Gass's Spindle Diagrams, which chart sound and rhythm as opposed to syntactical movement, seem to be sending out shoots of some sort, but they are more like the understory of a forest than erect trees.

SPINDLE DIAGRAM—SOUND AND RHYTHM PATTERN

From James Joyce, *Finnegans Wake,* conclusion.

		[oh]				
And	it's	old				
and		old				
	it's			sad		
and		old				
	it's			sad		
and				weary		
[that]	I	go			back	to you,
	my	cold				father,
	my	cold	mad	feary		father,
till	the			near	sight	
of	the			mere	size	of him,
	the			moyles		
and				moyles		of it,
				moan-		
				an-		
				oan-		
				ing,		
makes me				seasilt		
				saltsick		
and	I			rush,		
		my only,				into your arms.

73

After expatriating herself, Gertrude Stein stayed away for over thirty years. When she did return, it was to deliver several lectures, one of which, "Poetry and Grammar," fondly recalls her childhood of sentence diagramming. "When you are at school and learn grammar grammar is very exciting. I really do not know that anything has ever been more exciting than diagramming sentences. I suppose other things may be more exciting to others when they are at school but to me undoubtedly when I was at school the really completely exciting thing was diagramming sentences and that has been to me ever since the one thing that has been completely exciting and completely completing. I like the feeling the everlasting feeling of sentences as they diagram themselves."

Thanks to today's many computer-generated parsing programs, sentences really seem to diagram themselves, but the joy is lost. It is true that the most straight-forward of these new trees, which are reminiscent of a Calder mobile, manage to relate some of the principles of balance often found in the "successful" sentence. But the sentences lack character. Despite the fact that I have searched Treebank after Treebank, Parsed Corpus after Parsed Corpus, the wood is never green, the body no longer living.

These new trees break down along the lines of either constituency or dependency, though one can create a hybrid tree. Glancing at such trees, we see,

visually,

that hierarchy has replaced multidirectionality.

Nonetheless, I find I cannot leave off without including the results of at least one of the many on-line diagramming applications I performed. Having submitted the original sentence—"I feel so Americanly close to Jones Very, so tenderly tied to the tragedy of marriage (incest?) and madness"—to Version 4.0: A Phrase-Parser. I was given the following gifts, a chart of linkages and a constituent tree:

```
+--------MX*p-------+----------
    +----------Pa----------+   +----Js---+ +-------Xd-------+  +----J
 +-Sp*i+  +-------EAxk------+--MVp-+  +--G--+ | +-EExk+---Em--+-MVp+ +--

 |  |  |      |  |  |  |  || |   |  ||  |
I.p feel.v so [Americanly] close.a to Jones Very , so tenderly tied.v to the

-------------------Xc----------------------------+
p---+   +-------Jp-------+           |
D*u-+--Mp--+   +----AN---+           |
 |  |  |  |         |
tragedy.n of marriage.n incest.n and madness.n RIGHT-WALL


              +--------MX*p-------+----------
    +----------Pa----------+   +----Js---+ +-------Xd-------+  +----J
 +-Sp*i+  +-------EAxk------+--MVp-+  +--G--+ | +-EExk+---Em--+-MVp+ +--
 |  |  |      |  |  |  || |   |  ||  |
I.p feel.v so [Americanly] close.a to Jones Very , so tenderly tied.v to the


-------------------Xc----------------------------+
p---+                |
D*u-+--Mp--+---------------Jp-------------+    |
 |  |          |  |
tragedy.n of marriage.n incest.n and madness.n RIGHT-WALL
```

Constituent tree:

```
(S (NP I)
 (VP feel
  (ADJP (ADVP so)
    Americanly close
    (PP to
     (NP Jones Very
      (VP ,
       (ADVP so tenderly)
       tied
       (PP to
        (NP (NP the tragedy)
         (PP of
          (NP (NP marriage incest)
           and
           (NP madness)))))))))))
```

I discovered the poet Jones Very accidentally, though I don't recall where or how. I do know it was his name that struck a cord, so excessively of itself. A child of first cousins, his given name was his father's, his surname his parents'. Consanguine marriage wasn't illegal in the United States until after the Civil War, and Very, living as he was on either side of the split that joined us, was not technically the offspring of incest. I recently read that some 80 percent of marriages across history have been between second cousins or closer. And aren't our first sexual experiences so often with our cousins? The only people who would call those exploratory-bunk-bed-romps incest are adolescent counselors desperate to offer explanations to concerned parents and even more desperate to find some need for extended, overpriced therapy. The closest Old English comes to the word "incest" is "sibliger," which simply means "kin-lying."

And yet Very respected no figure more than Hamlet, who was, he said, the noblest of Shakespeare's characters, the only one left to consider questions of being. "With us, to be rich or not to be rich, to be wise or not to be wise, to be honored or not to be honored,— those are the questions."

> As if an auxiliary verb
> must always serve
> some other word.

No other character, Very says, better reflects Shakespeare's own character. Hamlet's mother married "with such dexterity to incestuous sheets!" Not because she married her own blood, but because she was lying with, to, and about kin.

Brothers Isaac Very and Samuel Very, Jones's grandfathers, were seamen, as was his own father, the first Jones Very. But the younger Jones, having sailed with his father for over a year, returned to land with no interest in setting sail again.

Despite their shared blood and maritime occupations, there was a curious chasm between the Very families. When the elder Jones Very died, leaving behind his wife-cousin, Lydia Very, and their four children, his father, Isaac Very, tried to claim what little money the younger Jones had left. Isaac Very accused his niece-cum-daughter-in-law of concealing, embezzling or conveying away some Twelve-hundred and fifty dollars, an unspecified amount of gold, and the deceased's quadrant, sextant and spyglass. Lydia Very insisted she never found the money, and intimated that she believed the gold was stolen by her own aunt-mother-in-law. As for the celestial navigation instruments, Lydia Very told a court of law, "I was his wife and these were his children, and I thought we had the best right to them."

In-law
the court agreed.

THE COLUMBINE.

STILL, still my eye will gaze long fixed on thee,
Till I forget that I am called a man,
And at thy side fast-rooted seem to be,
And the breeze comes my cheek with thine to fan.
Upon this craggy hill our life shall pass,
A life of summer days and summer joys,
Nodding our honey-bells mid pliant grass
In which the bee half hid his time employs;
And here we'll drink with thirsty pores the rain,
And turn dew-sprinkled to the rising sun,
And look when in the flaming west again
His orb across the heaven its path has run;
Here left in darkness on the rocky steep,
My weary eyes shall close like folding flowers in sleep.

No Melville, the sea hardly ever serves a subject for Very, and when it does but once or twice, as in "The Sight of the Ocean," Very's lines are as weary as his ocean wave:

> The plaintive wave, as it broke on the shore,
> Seemed sighing for rest forevermore.

But in Very's eyes, the waves of Walden Pond did not tire of their lonesome activity; rather, they were in chorus and crescendo with one another. Very once asked Emerson to look out over the pond and "see how each wave rises from the midst with an original force, at the same time that it partakes the general movement.'"

Very seems himself to be describing himself, a wave in the Transcendental sea, one that rose originary, but lent and borrowed its force freely. During his first visit with the Transcendental Club in May 1838, Very apparently spoke so eloquently that Bronson Alcott declared, "as if, in answer to the inquiry whether Mysticism was an element of Christianity, here was an illustration of it in living person, himself present at the club."

Elizabeth Peabody and Nathaniel Hawthorne, Very's Salem neighbors, both admitted his genius, the latter writing, in 1842, "Jones Very, a poet whose voice is scarcely heard among us by reason of its depth, there was a Wind Flower and a Columbine." Very had almost 40 more years of life ahead of him, and yet "there [he] was." Is such playfulness with tense prophecy? I own every columbine I can hold. When I bought my first Colorado home, I pulled what I thought was a weed, and now I see its resilient seed, first to bloom through the fire. The flower has two names too. Not just columbine, which means dove, its bloom resembling five doves huddled together from above, but also *Aquilegia*, Latin for eagle, the petals its claw.

If you want the flower, and not the school shooting, you must indicate as much in your search.

A voice scarcely heard.

& the poem harder to find still.

Perhaps Hawthorne renames Very the very names of his poems because, in them, he forgets his own name. He doesn't forget he is a man; he forgets he is called one, and such forgetting is the beginning of assuming another name. Still, still he seems to be born in this poem, and he surely dies here, in the flaming west. But slowly, with one extra foot in the final line, so that flowers may be folding.

But it was Emerson who devoted the most attention to his "brave saint." As many times as I have read Emerson's "Friendship," I never knew Very was the man who made every other man see society's "face and eye" rather than its "side and back." It was Very who prompted Emerson to ask, "To stand in true relations with men in a false age is worth a fit of insanity, is it not?"

Very's fit of insanity took the form of prophecy. As a professor of Greek at Harvard, Very had an unwitting audience for his devout sentiments. For eighteen months, he cultivated complete will-lessness, the results of which were rapid weight loss and over three-hundred ecstatic poems taken directly from the mouth of God. But, it wasn't until he stood before his students and urged them to "flee to the mountains, for the end of all things is at hand," that he was dismissed from Harvard and admitted into the McLean Asylum for the Insane.

When the diagnosed seems not too concerned with the diagnoses, is it evidence of madness or sanity? While in the Asylum, Very finished his essay on Hamlet, in which he compared the Prince of Denmark to the apostle Paul: "Like the vision-struck Paul, in the presence of Felix, he spoke what to those around him, whose eyes had not been opened on that light brighter than the sun, seemed madness; but which was, in fact, the words of truth and soberness."

> "divinest sense," says Dickinson
> "such a mind cannot be lost," says Emerson

Perhaps you've heard of the McLean Asylum before. Sylvia Plath, Anne Sexton, Robert Lowell, siblings James, Kate, and Livingston Taylor, Ray Charles, Steven Tyler, David Foster Wallace, Zelda Fitzgerald, and a dozen other famous writers, musicians, scientists, and mathematicians took their rest-cures in this extravagant hospital for the rich.

Fredrick Law Olmstead contributed to the design of the facilities, and then he was treated there. It is impossible to say for sure, but it appears as though William James spent time at the asylum as well. In his *Varieties of Religious Experience*, James offers an example of what he calls "panic fear," attributing it to a French patient who spent time in an unnamed asylum. According to James's translation of the patient's account ("I translate freely," James writes), one evening having entered a dark room, the patient experienced a great fear of his existence while simultaneously recalling the image of an epileptic man he had seen during his stay in the asylum. The patient reports: "This image and my fear entered into a species of combination with each other. *That shape I am,* I felt, potentially."

And, as it turns out, that shape he was. When translating *The Varieties of Religious Experience* into French, the translator, Frank Abauzit, wrote to James in hopes of securing this account in its original French. James replied, "the document is my own case . . . . so you may translate freely."

By *species*, does James simply mean a kind of combination, or does he mean vision? It is hard not to bring to bear so many other things here,

such as, species means:

        appearance,
        reflection,

a thing seen,
a common quality,
human and all other living things,
distinct

But it also means, to Socrates at least, idea. It is no cogito but it is existence. The
word meaning meaning.

When God says, "I am that I am," maybe he simply means, "I am *that* I am." God
being cheeky, showing Moses just how slippery language can be, particularly
words that point at pointing, like *this* and like *that*, I am that iamb

this that

he riddles our riddle back to us

"What I like most about God," my daughter tells me, "is his stories"; after a pause the pierce of a semicolon, she demands, "And now you tell me one." One of the most exhausting things about parenting is meeting children's endless demands on your imagination. A friend, at her wits' end, calls me and admits, "if I have to talk behind another stuffed animal for even one minute longer, I don't know what I'll do." I suggest she cut the head off her daughter's stuffed bunny, holding its body up to hers, all the while continuing to narrate so that the transformation of mommy into bunny might itself be a kind of cure.

My children clamor after story.

hours and hours of telling stories while driving (to & from school), doing dishes, cooking, serving (breakfast, lunch, dinner & snack), shopping, bathing, brushing (teeth & hair), dressing (children, babydolls & stuffed animals), fastening, unfastening (seatbelts & buttons), wiping (noses, faces, hands & asses), drawing, taping, folding (paper & clothing), packing (lunchboxes, diaper bags & backpacks), spelling, naming, fixing, walking (for pleasure & in a hurry), tying, zipping, velcroing (coats, jeans & shoes), cutting (paper & hair), administering (lotion, medicine & discipline) all the while

I attempt to avoid formulas, but children define stories by their constituents, so that each story must include a baby, an injured pet, and a near-fatal accident. I challenge myself to carry on in ways that are themselves childlike—continue until a red car passes, or the mailman crosses the street, or a child has to pee. After awhile, everything I say is stolen from the bedtime stories I was told, or rather, read. Mothers as backhoes, rabbits among the brambles, run-away children, tired of living in houses, chased home, finally, by the elements.

Eventually, I offer simply an article and a noun, insisting we tell stories in rounds.

Their verb: poops.

Or, I suggest, you tell me a story instead.

I cannot, the youngest says, I'm allowing my brain to rest.

And yet we all invent devices for filling up the crevices and disguising the fissures.

Something Homer once said proves itself true again and again. That is, wine tempts one to blurt out stories better never told. In other words, rather than thinking ahead, it seems I am forever comforting them so that they might stay in their beds.

Every night for 30 nights, I have a strange and moving dream. Our house kindly builds upon itself a second story, spacious and open, into which only I can climb.

I never planned to follow the poems on water with a poem on fire. The water poems were meant to be erotic, an everyday investigation of intimacy. It occurred to me, after teaching Whitman's bathing scene, that poetry might know the watering hole where *cogito* and *coitus* meet, the one that warmly aches, or gently vibrates, like the hymen, or, more accurately, the spot where the hymen was previously. I've come to associate this cavity with the number thirty, the ruptured tissue a three, the whole hole a zero, a 0, or perhaps an O.

If you perform an online search for the word "hymen," you'll learn that this vaginal membrane is "a source of confusion, even 'myth' for a lot of people." Myth, indeed. For virgins and their first lovers, this is a place of mystery to which we cling

until, like Catullus, we sing:

> *Hymenaeus Hymen, come! O Hymen Hymenaeus!*
> *Hymenaeus Hymen, come! O Hymen Hymenaeus!*

& he does, tall, says Sappho,

whence womb-fury

> *'Tis Hymen peoples every town*

he tells Phebe

> *& now a hymn she sings me.*

I wanted to be the number thirty, the thirtieth bather, the age when Jesus started his ministry, the number of silver pieces Judas received. But it was the beginning of Lent, and I had given up sex. I suppose I had hoped, as Dante had, to transform my carnal love into a new life devoted, as the case might be, to Christianity. When Dante's "tongue of love" speaks,

"the sight of her is humbling to all things"

By day thirty, I was as if blind. I sat at God's feet, but coitus interuptus as it so often does.

Hymen, the Gr god of marriage; **hymen,** the virginal membrane broken during the consummation of marriage; **hymeneal,** of or by or for or at (a) wedding, a marriage; cf the element *hymeno-*;— **hymn,** orig a bridal song, hence a song of praise, esp of Deity; **hymnal** (adj, hence n), **hymnary, hymnody** (whence **hymnodist**), **hymnology** (whence **hymnologist**).

By the way, the blow-job scene in *Song of Myself* is fun to teach. After one class, I received a handwritten, twice folded note from a student that read, "you seem to agree with every student but me." This surprises me because though I often experience great satisfaction while teaching, or rather, after teaching, I never think of it as the satisfaction of agreement. In the classroom, I rarely feel that I agree with anyone but me, and yet they let me teach. By "they" I don't mean the administration, or even the students, though I am often shocked when an hour passes and no one gets up to leave. Sometimes, in the classroom, I imagine the ground below me crawling, teeming even, with its own authority. *They* is the earth that lets me

but I promised not

to write on yet

another element

though, as Keats once said,

the poetry of earth is never dead

and this poem is for itself itself its own death.

It is a watershed. That is, what the earth does with its elements. The mountains on fire, waters ashore up and down the seaboard, higher and higher. I suppose someone once said the word *fire-souled,* and from it pliant sandals of fire-cured skin, wood being what allows us to speak without speaking aloud.

The will will will itself away.

In 1838, Jones Very visited Elizabeth Peabody. Looking much flushed, he laid his hands on her head and said, "I come to baptize you with the Holy Ghost and with Fire." He claimed his poems were fire-baptized as well, but Emerson saw flaws and asked,

> "cannot the spirit parse & spell?"

Emerson thought Very "profoundly sane."

From my tree, I see three fire-spouts broke out. I want all wildlife inside me.
> Wildfire, o oath

> I have broken.

An oath is an incident that is more than incidental but less than fundamental, the difference between the promise and what is promised. Agamben says an oath binds word and action, making it both curse and blessing, blessing if the word is full, curse if the word is empty. The gods' first oath is water, the river Styx, life on one side, and on the other, the other. Even when God says, "by myself have I sworn," he means by the water.

& the blessing be the seed multiplied

as

the sand by the sea shore

the stars in the sky

the blessing be the offspring aplenty, the offspring too many.

There are some things that illustrate others without being anything at all. I've watched and watched those lessen in number. Blindsided, the sound of pigeons above the sea seems to make a shape like longing. In plain sight, daylight. People often say, *watch and learn* or some version thereof. I try to say, upon occasion, something quite opposite. Upon, occasion. I try also to see what happens when the nested prepositional phrase learns it can, with the help of even the most dismal wind, fly. To move it beyond simply an accessory. But being weary, it finally occurs to me to release it instead, to unleash it on some untrodden patch, some tangle, some mess of bluegrass, some stockpile of trees. Trees which know better our needs. Horkos, depending on who you ask, means also "sacred substance."

"cursed is everyone that hangeth on a tree"

Having sown, I sit and watch the common oat grow

                                            reverberant,

riverbent.

Aflame, it itself made

"redeemed from fire by fire"
—T. S. ELIOT

This is a world
very wolved

        different from yesterday's
        and already begun to cool

as if
it could be

        dismissed
        I stand

in the burning field
look back and see grief

        where wheat
        won't grow.

To thrive I've,
we've, all of us

        it seems
        lived in extremes

all of us always
need privacy

        this neighborly
        edeneternal

has its boundaries
of bindweed

                              and cacti
                              on this side of the cliff

not at all
touched by it.

                              Still, it seems
                              raging right here

not a bird in the air
the world a fruit

                              to do with it
                              and through it

what He will
fog without fail

                              the house, an island
                              of ash and I imagine

a blanket of snow
falling still

                              slowly watering,
                              wintering in reverse

air aqueous
a waterwall

100 houses
follow.

*

In this world of poem
I can only do what is undone

each movement
stands in for moments

unimagining lightning
imagining a lightening

auroras like cypresses
geomagnetic storms

ornaments
a kindling of the eye

as it shuts before opening
the very first time.

I'm looking for flourishing
I take it in my hands

                                        flour, the breadth
                                        opens alphabets

they hardly stir
to quench it

                                        it finds thoughts
                                        thoughts find

their place
and place

                                        themselves not in line
                                        but along the ridge we walk

so cleanly done
it could not be human

                                        it a word we try not to use
                                        so useful now

it opens it
a promethean gift-theft

                                        is still a gift
                                        fennel-stock of heat

bull bones in glistening fat
beef hides

                                        inside an ox's stomach
                                        all clay again for the making.

That which
survives it

                                        it made
                                        it fired this pot

it melded this metal
meanwhile
                                        all else
                                        else

*

Unspecified *it*
the formal imperative

                                        up the stunning stairwell
                                        and out

the house
vividly arrested

                                        drops off a cliff
                                        above the tree line

the never summer range
remain

                    waters suddenly
                    flowing the other way

back from where they came
path and endpost

                    gate, forever opens
                    greets

heat, all but heat
is symbolic

                    and thus, all but heat
                    is reductive

it takes the waters
as reins

                    it follows waves
                    it holds its own breastplate

it breathes
it sees its

                    feet stepping forward
                    out before it it needs embrace

it a thousand leaved
red root pigweed

it cannot be
anything other than

beauty,
its own face raging

it's bravery
each tool

we yield against it
forged by it

it has a name
which it does not exhaust

or receive
it does not admit it

plurality of seeds beneath
it winded it

toward it
ananke, flag of necessity.

*

too soon it took its foot away
it it without name

from whence it came?

*

or rather,
from whom it flamed?

the iguana carried it
in its head-crest

the flame-tailed finch,
behind its back

the cockatoo,
in her red chest

the water-rat and cod-fish
hid it in their thickets

dogs with burning sticks
on their tails swam the straight

the musk-duck
the crocodile's mouth

the wallaroo
issuing forth from his penis

little boys and old ladies
with flaming fingers

                                             pointed at it
                                             with it

bird-thieves: woodpeckers,
kingfishers, hummingbirds & hawks

                                             tigers pulling throngs
                                             from their claws.

The sloth carried it
between his shoulders

                                             the coyote brought it
                                             on her hair.

The guinea pig
stole it from the jaguar

                                             the toad
                                             from the vulture

the deaf adder
released it when he laughed

                                             thanks to the dancing deer
                                             with combustible

weeds
in her ears.

The caribou hid it
in her headdress

the beaver
in his watercourses

the muskrat in her apron
of marmot skin.

A spider,
having spun a large web

upon which a woodpecker
pecked,

extended a thin but sturdy ladder
to our castor and pollux.

Or, the same spider,
by way of a gossamer balloon,

brought it back
from the moon.

May I present
the robin's red breast

as evidence of fire
in her chest.

*

But before that
in the smoke

of hoariest history
the sun

moved tidal
and temporal

answering
with tinder

my feather stick
of thin curls

hewed
by love.

I find live timber
not a weapon

but a welcome
a settler's blessing.

The black war was
a misunderstanding

                               mariners saw a musket
                               not a wisp of straw

not an aboriginal offering
but gates of basalt.

                               The heart like
                               a covered flame

sings as it is consumed
agnis agile ignis ire

                               little white flower
                               noble blue center

reddens when tossed
over the precipice

                               royalty evidenced:
                               both laurel trees & lion bones

when shaken, spark
scarf of earth

                               auburn auburned
                               crown crowned

the treetops with fire
with ebon honor.

*

Do you know
what happens when

one story falls
upon another?

what happens to bathtubs?
to beds?

what happens
to chimneys?

Let's see how to tell
it without it

consuming us.
It says, gather beside me

as you have for centuries
tell instead the dream

of the deceased
each of each

carrying one unharmed belonging
down the mountain

                              before the flame inflames
                              the alembic of the world

not dreamed
spindle and weave

                              H.D.'s burnt tree
                              & how the wind does carry

without barrier
not the seed, but the thread

                              mustard's edible leaves
                              I wear a dress of these

· newly picked
encyclopedic

                              of the soil
                              incombustible

the forest's understory
speaks,

                              says, verily
                              I say unto thee

today
you will be with me.

*

We must be
in disaster

                                        occasionally
                                        its winds

not tragedy not
the kind that cannot

                                        be overcome
                                        but the coming kind.

We all have it in common
one long longing

                                        to see it renewed
                                        it touches our body

this tree's obituary
viewed collectively

                                        and what is community but
                                        connectivity held loosely

the pond not burned
to the ground

                                because it is the ground
                                the deer standing

safe in its center
and so much easier now to see

                                the dark place we've
                                lived so long alight

wolves in their sanctuary
foxes in their dens

                                we position ourselves
                                wonder what burnt first

& from which direction
we photograph

                                though no one photo
                                can hold it

the child, hopeful, says
there may be a corner left

                                yes,
                                there may be astral radiance

this little grassy tussock
not an accident

all but Antarctica
melts in its presence.

*

Streams of silver
where the lawnchair

once was
the playset remains

untouched
it calms us

& in its face
we see relief

we see it
for what it is:

able-bodied it
it itself makes

the word
& its worship.

*

At the point of the fl
ame if

the sword lilies
are phototropic

where gladiolas'
if

color gives way
to an invisible

vibration it rains if
a sterile land shimme

little safeling
ring

if ash
en it rains

a little
on the tinder

if tend
er larval

if the dream
gives for

m to that never be
fore dreamed but live

d, if livid
look it in the face

far distance
holy for

est where color
gives way t

o shade
if

it is a
flame

we be
for it

long
ing.

*

We brush it
and see if anything shines.

No thing does
but embers

& the black backs
of our beetles.

It floods us
in emblems

it is
not an element

but an event
like slaughtering

a rooster
where there's room

and no thing
to ruin.

I've said
my prayers

the land is
a mushroom

a morel
honeycombed

hive of the world
and only growing

because it
spread its arms wide.

It held
the lodgepole pine

whose needles
need heat to reseed

the tree
where the imagined

and the discovered
meet

it, fire
a gift

however mercurial
is irenic

always plural
surrounded by itself

it is
never singular

it lisps
perhaps we'll learn

from this
very word   earth

                    to sing
                    what we serve.

The first epigraph was translated from Middle English by Jorie Graham:

Earth Took of Earth

Earth took of earth earth with ill;
Earth other earth gave earth a will.
Earth laid earth in the earth stock-still:
Then earth in earth had of earth its fill.

This poem first appeared in 1307, though it was most certainly written a few centuries before. Some even say it was adapted from Latin. When reading this poem in Middle English, we see what we know but sometimes forget—our words are ambivalent. Is "ynoh" (enough) excessive or sufficient? Is "oþer" beyond or other, or is it over? Despite the fact that the original poem was without title, different editors have titled the poem variously—Did earth take of itself (to make itself, perhaps), as Graham's title insists; is it, as Charlton Brown suggests in his anthology of thirteenth-century English lyrics, a matter of transference from one earth to another—"From Earth to Earth;" or is it a layering—"Earth upon Earth"—as Hilda Murray offers in her exhaustive study of the poem's twenty-four appearances? The answer to these questions is a non-answer—it is both and other, and it is none. It is untitled. The earth gives, takes, and makes, to and from and for us, and to and from and for itself.

The dailiness of *Waters: A Lenten Poem*, written over the course of the 40 days of Lent in 2012, demanded that I register several events, some national, some personal. The shooting at Charddon High School, the murder of Trayvon Martin, the GOP's war on women, the death of Adrienne Rich, and several birthdays are mentioned here. The poem also borrows language from a number of sources. Section 6 borrows from the Middle English Harley Lyric, "Lenten ys come wiþ loue to toune." The entirety of Section 9 is taken from Robert Herrick's "To Keep a True Lent," though I have omitted punctuation and removed all capitalization. Section 21 resurrects William Carlos Williams' line "with weight and urgency," a line he cut from "The Great Figure." All lines in Section 35 were culled from every 40th page of Adrienne Rich's collections: *An Atlas of the Difficult World: Poems 1988–1991* and *The Fact of a Doorframe: Poems Selected and New 1950–1984*.

I Couldn't Stop Watching was a conceptus before water and fire, but it is what came between, and after. There are many sources, most of which are obvious, and the rest of which I have likely forgotten.

Aflame, it Itself made was written during the month of June 2012 and revised during the month of June 2013. That first June, fires raged all over the country, but Colorado in particular was covered in a blanket of smoke. One day that month, my parents lost their house in the High Park Fire. As a result, shortly after finishing *Waters*, I found myself writing about fire. As poetry often knows before we do, I shored up what was needed to rest easy in the heat. Various writers including Charles Olson, D.H. Lawrence, and Paul-Jean Toulet, are quoted here, though without the quotation marks. In June 2013, as I revised, I watched from my bedroom window as smoke billowed above Rocky Mountain National Park.

SASHA STEENSEN is the author of three previous books: *House of Deer,* *The Method,* and *A Magic Book,* all from Fence Books. Recent work has appeared in *Kenyon Review, West Branch, Omniverse,* and *Dusie.* "Openings: Into Our Vertical Cosmos" was recently published as an online chapbook by Essay Press. She teaches Creative Writing and Literature at Colorado State University, where she also serves as a poetry editor for *Colorado Review.* She lives with her husband and two daughters, and she tends a garden, a flock of chickens, a barn cat, and two goats.

AHSAHTA PRESS

NEW SERIES

AHSAHTA PRESS

SAWTOOTH POETRY PRIZE SERIES

2002: Aaron McCollough, *Welkin* (Brenda Hillman, judge)
2003: Graham Foust, *Leave the Room to Itself* (Joe Wenderoth, judge)
2004: Noah Eli Gordon, *The Area of Sound Called the Subtone* (Claudia Rankine, judge)
2005: Karla Kelsey, *Knowledge, Forms, The Aviary* (Carolyn Forché, judge)
2006: Paige Ackerson-Kiely, *In No One's Land* (D. A. Powell, judge)
2007: Rusty Morrison, *the true keeps calm biding its story* (Peter Gizzi, judge)
2008: Barbara Maloutas, *the whole Marie* (C. D. Wright, judge)
2009: Julie Carr, *100 Notes on Violence* (Rae Armantrout, judge)
2010: James Meetze, *Dayglo* (Terrance Hayes, judge)
2011: Karen Rigby, *Chinoiserie* (Paul Hoover, judge)
2012: T. Zachary Cotler, *Sonnets to the Humans* (Heather McHugh, judge)
2013: David Bartone, *Practice on Mountains* (Dan Beachy-Quick, judge)
2014: Aaron Apps, *Dear Herculine* (Mei-mei Berssenbrugge, judge)
2015: Vincent Toro, *Stereo. Island. Mosaic.* (Ed Roberson, judge)
2016: Jennifer Nelson, *Civilization Makes Me Lonely* (Anne Boyer, judge)

THIS BOOK IS SET IN APOLLO MT TYPE
WITH PERPETUA STANDARD TITLES
BY AHSAHTA PRESS AT BOISE STATE UNIVERSITY.
COVER DESIGN BY QUEMADURA.
BOOK DESIGN BY JANET HOLMES.

AHSAHTA PRESS
2017

JANET HOLMES, DIRECTOR

LINDSEY APPELL
PATRICIA BOWEN, *intern*
MICHAEL GREEN
KATHRYN JENSEN
COLIN JOHNSON
MATT NAPLES